Expanded of the Method for Converting Shipping Containers into a Habitable Steel Building

Expanded discussion of the 1989 Clark shipping container building method patent. Contains new illustrations and ideas based on the steel shipping container structures and building methods originally described.

Paul Sawyers Publications

Expanded Discussion of the Method for Converting Shipping Containers into a Habitable Steel Building

ISBN-10: 1463532113
ISBN-13: 978-1463532116

This publication is based on the description provided for United States Patent "Method for converting one or more steel shipping containers into a habitable building at a building site and the product thereof". Original text and images from the patent description, accompanied by new supplemental text and images, are presented within this publication. The publisher of this book is not affiliated in any way with the United States Patent and Trademark Office, or the patent inventor Phillip C. Clark.

Patent number: 4854094
Filing date: Nov 23, 1987
Issue date: Aug 8, 1989
Inventor: Phillip C. Clark

United States Patent and Trademark Office Editorial Standards, Publications and Citations

Copyrights are administered by the Copyright Office, a division of the Library of Congress. Copyright law (17 U.S.C. § 105) states that all materials created by the United States government are in the public domain. However, there are restrictions on use. Anyone incorporating a work of the U.S. Government into a copyrighted work should be aware of 17 U.S. C. § 403 . This section requires a copyright notice to contain a statement identifying what portions of the work consist of a work of the U.S. Government. Failure to do so could result in loss of copyright protection for the entire work.

Patents are published as part of the terms of granting the patent to the inventor. Subject to limited exceptions reflected in 37 CFR 1.71(d) & (e) and 1.84(s) , the text and drawings of a patent are typically not subject to copyright restrictions. The inventors' right to exclude others from making, using, offering for sale, or selling the invention throughout the United States or importing the invention into the United States for a limited time is not compromised by the publication of the description of the invention. In other words, the fact that a patent's description may have been published without copyright restrictions does not give you permission to manufacture or use the invention without permission from the inventor during the active life of the patent.

The following portions of this publication contain text or images from the United States Patent and Trademark Office (original description of patent number 4854094): Written content on pages 7-16, 18-30, 33-34, 38-52, and back cover. Illustrations on page 7, 17, 18, 20, 22, 24, 26, 28, 30, 34, 41, 43, 45, 47, 49, 51, and 53.

Raw shipping container models provided by sketchup.google.com/3dwarehouse
Shipping container 20' by Google, and Shipping container 40' by Google.

The 3D building models shown in this book can be downloaded at www.paulsawyers.com

Contents

Preface

In 1987 Phillip C. Clark filed a patent describing several basic methods for assembly of shipping container structures. The buildings are designed to be used in a utilitarian nature on construction and industrial sites mainly for storage, offices, or perhaps even temporary lodging and shelter.

The Clark Shipping Container Building Patent...

"Method for converting one or more steel shipping containers into a habitable building at a building site and the product thereof"

Patent number: 4854094
Filing date: Nov 23, 1987
Issue date: Aug 8, 1989
Inventor: Phillip C. Clark

While many in the shipping container or construction industry may have prior knowledge of this patents existence, it remains largely overlooked by modern shipping container building aficionados. It is not clear how this patent was used during it's active years, but it has since expired and is now in the public domain.

The Clark patent method describes using 2-3 steel shipping containers for creating habitable buildings. The patent also describes use of lumber built roofs to protect the structures, and several other essential basic techniques for creating successful buildings from standard twenty and forty foot steel shipping containers.

This expanded version of the patent description is presented as a study supplement for today's container building enthusiast.

1 The Invention

Method comprises mounting at least one standard steel shipping container on a weight-bearing foundation at the ends thereof. Where two or more containers are used, the containers may be in spaced and/or abutting side-by-side relationship; and/or may be mounted one upon another. Where containers are mounted side-by-side, portions of the inner sidewalls are removed leaving at least narrow flanges extending inwardly from the edges thereof. A roof is installed over the top walls of the containers; a raised floor is installed over the bottom walls of the containers enclosing flanges that extend inwardly from the bottom walls; and a dropped ceiling is installed under the top walls of the containers enclosing flanges that extend inwardly from the top walls. At least one window opening and one door opening are provided in the side and end walls, and a window and a door are installed therein. The invention includes the novel product of the method.

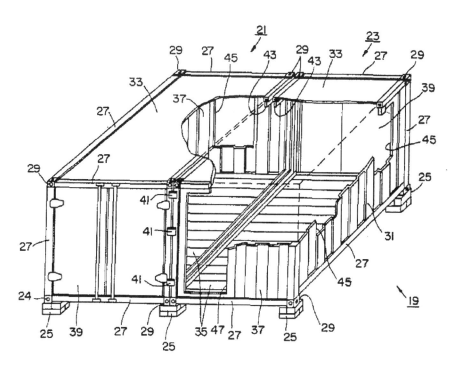

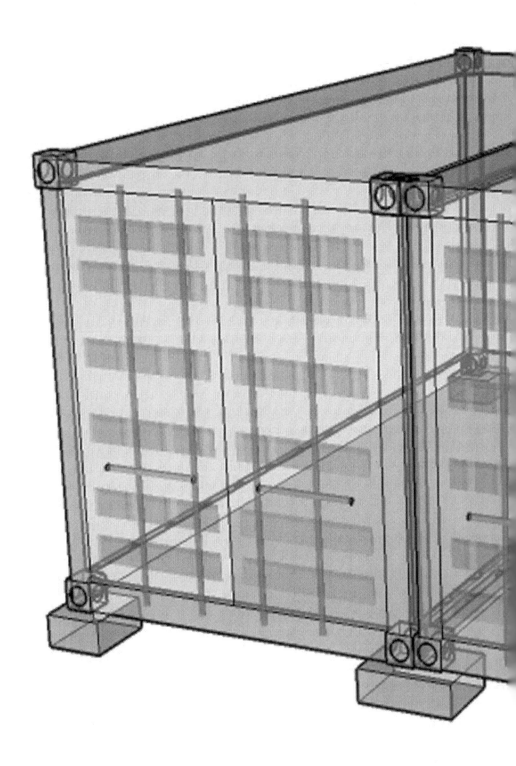

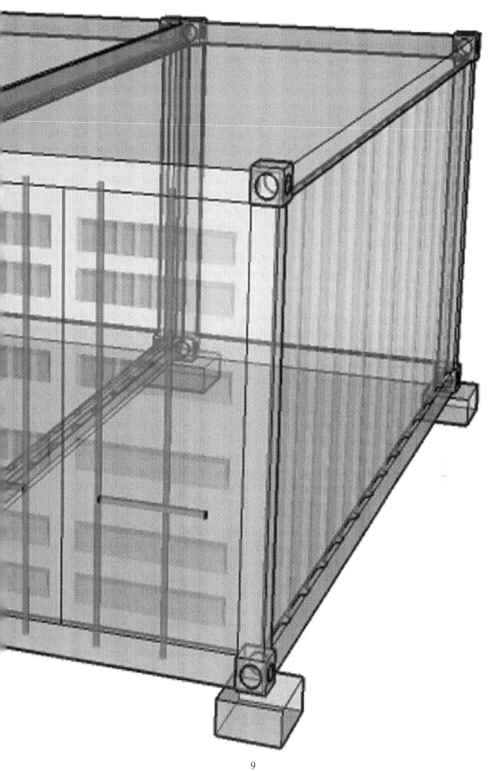

Background of the Invention

1. Field of the Invention

This invention relates to a novel method for converting one or more steel shipping containers to a habitable building. The novel method is carried out at the site where the building is to be used. The invention includes also the novel building produced by the novel method.

2. Description of the Prior Art

Much freight is now shipped overseas in containers of standard sizes; usually eight and one half (81/2) feet high, eight (8) feet wide and twenty (20) or forty (40) feet long. Marine freight is transported in steel containers that have a box-like frame of steel members, a bottom wall of steel channel beams attached to the frame and wood slats wedged there-between, a top wall, two opposed sidewalls of corrugated steel sheets welded to the frame, and two opposed steel end walls connected to the frame, one end wall of which includes two outwardly swinging steel doors. Each corner of the frame includes a special metal fitting adapted to pass a steel cable there-through. These fittings are used for lifting and lowering the container and for anchoring the containers to one another to prevent shifting and toppling in their transport vehicle.

These steel containers are very strong. However, after considerable use, they become uneconomical to use as shipping containers and they are taken out of service. The present invention seeks to use the residual characteristics of such used steel containers to produce habitable buildings economically.

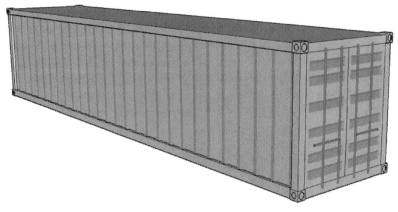

Prefabrication of buildings offers some advantages over on-site fabrication of new custom buildings, but the buildings are nevertheless expensive. The novel method does not involve prefabrication, although it enjoys some of the advantages attributed to prefabrication. The novel method takes advantage of the steel shipping containers that have been taken out of service and which can be converted at the building site to strong structural shells for buildings at low initial costs.

It is also known to convert shipping crates and tractor trailers into both temporary or permanent housing. The buildings produced by such conversions are relatively flimsy, flammable and relatively unsafe to be in. Conversions to such buildings are possible because of the light, structurally-weak character of the initial containers. The novel method converts standard steel shipping containers, which are structurally strong, and are not easily or obviously converted to safe, habitable buildings.

Objects of the Invention

Provide a novel method for converting one or more standard steel shipping containers into a habitable building.

Provide a method of the type described including the necessary steps for effecting such conversion.

Provide a method of the type described which is particularly adapted to be practiced at the site where the building is to be used.

Provide a method of the type described using steel shipping containers that have been used and taken out of service.

Provide a novel habitable building having, as its shell, one or more modified standard steel shipping containers.

Provide a habitable building having a novel construction and design.

Summary of the Invention

The above and related objects of this invention are achieved with the novel on-site method for converting one or more standard steel shipping containers into a habitable building. The novel method comprises mounting at least one such container on a weight-bearing foundation at the ends thereof. Where two or more containers are used, the containers may be in spaced and/or abutting side-by-side relationship; and/ or may be mounted one upon another. Where containers are mounted side-by-side, portions of the inner sidewalls are removed leaving at least narrow flanges extending inwardly from the edges thereof so as to retain most of the strength and rigidity of the containers. Openings are made in the outer sidewalls and the end walls for at least one window and one door, leaving at least a narrow inwardly-extending flange from the edges of the walls. A roof is installed over the top walls of the containers. A raised floor is installed over the bottom walls of the containers, which floor encloses any flanges extending inwardly from the bottom walls. A dropped ceiling is installed below the top walls of the containers, which ceiling encloses any flanges extending inwardly from the top walls. A window is installed in the window opening and a door is installed in the door opening.

The novel method takes advantage of the corrugated form of the sidewalls and endwalls of the steel containers so that they are treated in some respects as if they are stud walls as in residential frame house construction. The building may be further improved with the installation of thermal insulation, decorative inside walls, weather-resistant exterior covering, plumbing, electrical service, lighting, interior stud walls, etc. by novel steps that take advantage of the corrugated construction of the container walls, and/or by methods normally used in commercial and/or residential construction.

The novel method thereby uses the residual characteristics of out-of-service steel shipping containers, which containers are available all over the world at low cost. All of the materials needed in addition to the containers for the novel building may be placed within the containers to be modified and then be delivered to the building site. Thus, complete kits can be provided at minimal extra cost to the converter, and a reduced amount of building scrap is generated since the shipping container itself becomes part of the building. Of course, more than two containers may be joined in a horizontal array and, one or more containers may be stacked on top of the above-described array to produce any of various arrangements for a second level in the building. Also, another level of containers may be partially below ground level to provide a cellar for the building.

Hong Kong Marked Container Vessel in Seattle (photo Sam Rose)

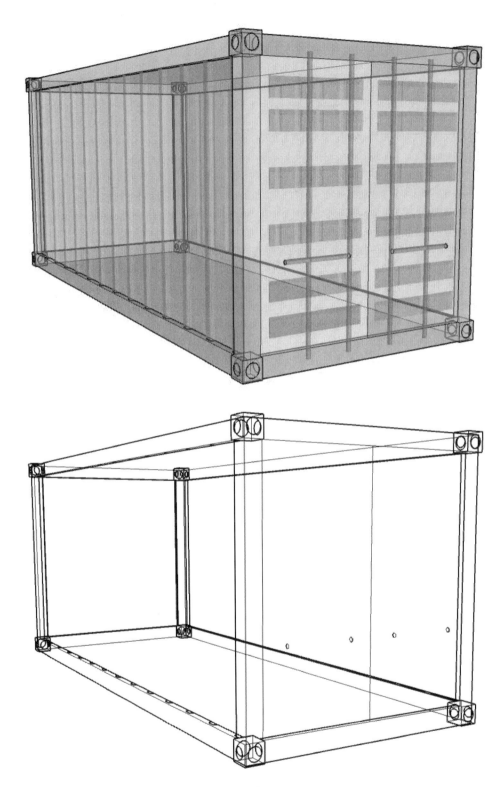

Forty Foot Shipping Container Building (photo Paul Sawyers)

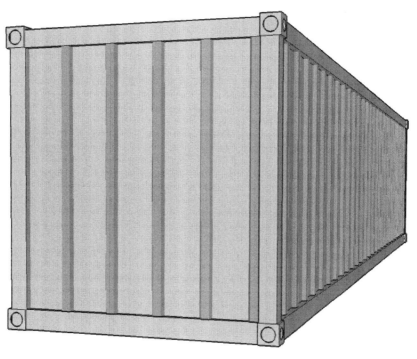

Claims

1. A habitable building comprising at least two steel shipping containers mounted on weight-bearing foundations located under endwalls and being joined together in adjacent, side-by-side relationship, the adjacent inner sidewalls having portions removed, with removed portions providing access between containers, a roof over and attached to the top walls of containers, a common raised floor over and attached to the bottom walls of containers, at least one window and at least one door in the walls of containers.

2. Alternative variation where substantially all of the inner adjacent sidewalls are removed from the containers.

3. Alternative variation including a common drop ceiling under top walls.

4. Alternative variation including finished inside walls attached to the inner surfaces of outer sidewalls and endwalls.

5. Alternative variation including finished outside walls attached to the outside surfaces of outer sidewalls and endwalls, with new finished outside walls including: a) an insulating layer adjacent to outside surfaces, b) a weather-resistant layer adjacent to insulating layer, and c) method of fastening weather-resistant layers to container walls.

The method for converting at least two, steel shipping containers into a habitable building, each container manufactured with a box-like frame of steel members, a bottom wall and a top wall connected to frame, two opposed steel sidewalls of corrugated steel sheets welded to frame, and two opposed endwalls connected to frame…

A. mounting at least two containers on weight-bearing foundations located under endwalls in adjacent, side-by-side relationship, joining containers together, and then carrying out the following steps:
B. removing facing portions of the adjacent inner sidewalls,
C. installing a roof over the top walls of containers,
D. installing a common raised floor over the bottom walls of containers,
E. providing at least one window opening and at least one door opening in the walls of containers, and
F. installing framework and a window in cut window opening and a door in cut door opening.

2 Patent Illustrations

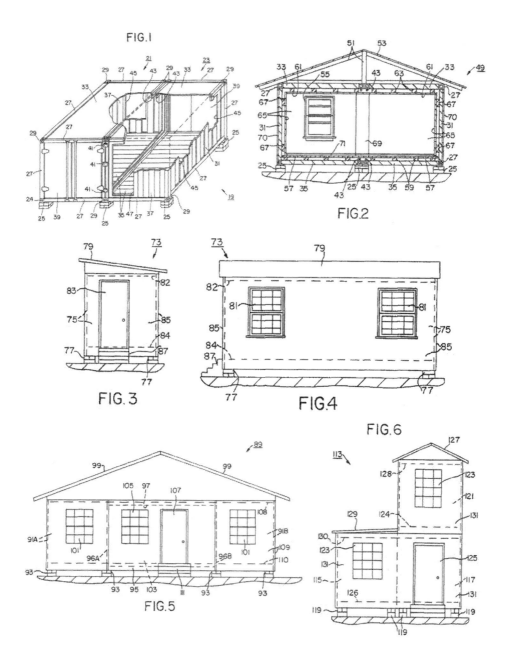

The original patent description includes seven black and white line drawn illustrations of shipping container buildings and the methods used for construction. This chapter will showcase these original illustrations in addition to modern renderings on each adjacent page.

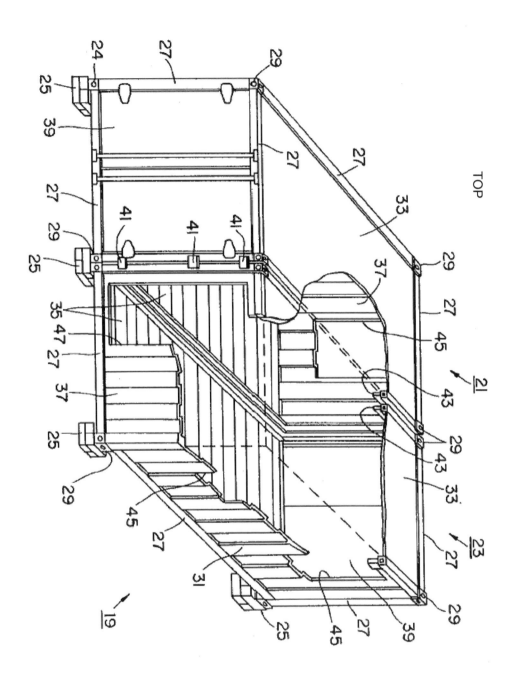

FIG. 1 is a broken-away perspective view of a first embodiment of a novel building at an intermediate stage of construction by the novel method with two steel containers in abutting, side-by-side relationship.

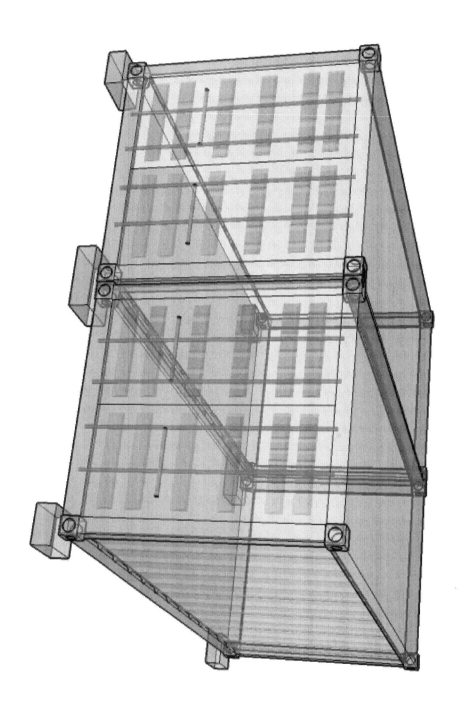

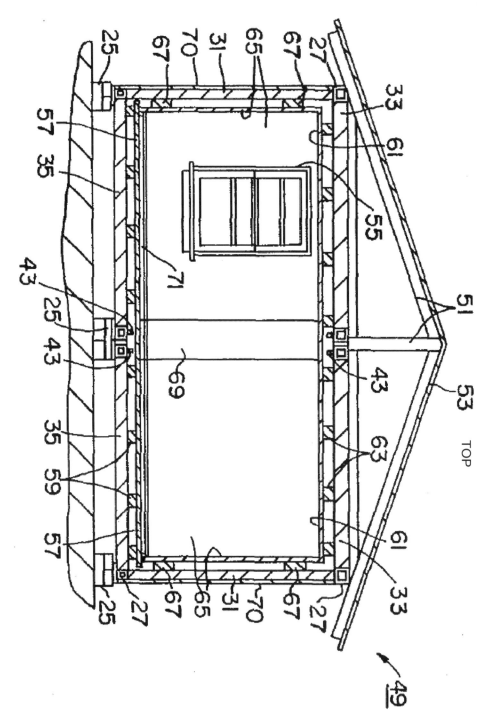

FIG. 2 is a sectional elevational view of a portion of the novel building shown in FIG. 1 after completion by the novel method.

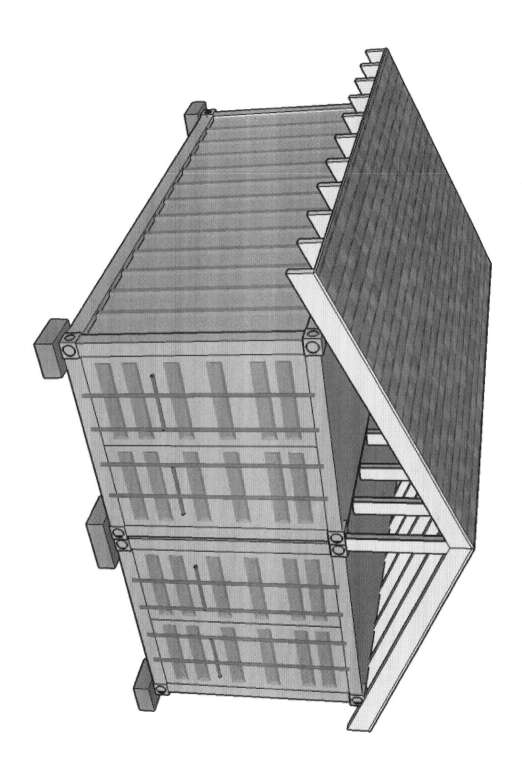

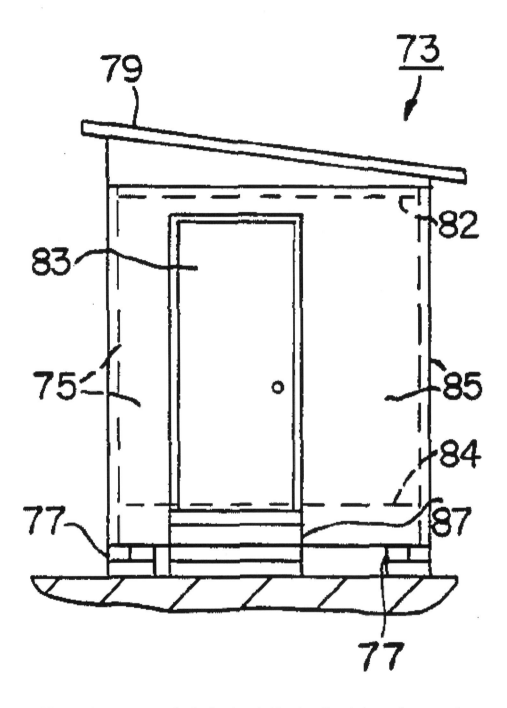

FIGS. 3 and 4 are, respectively, front and side elevational views of a second embodiment of a novel building prepared with only one steel container by the novel method.

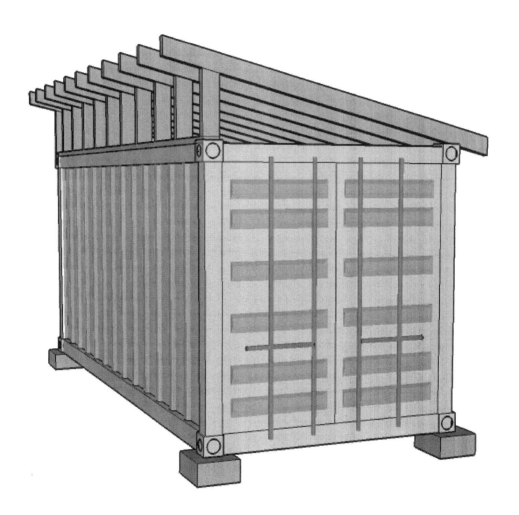

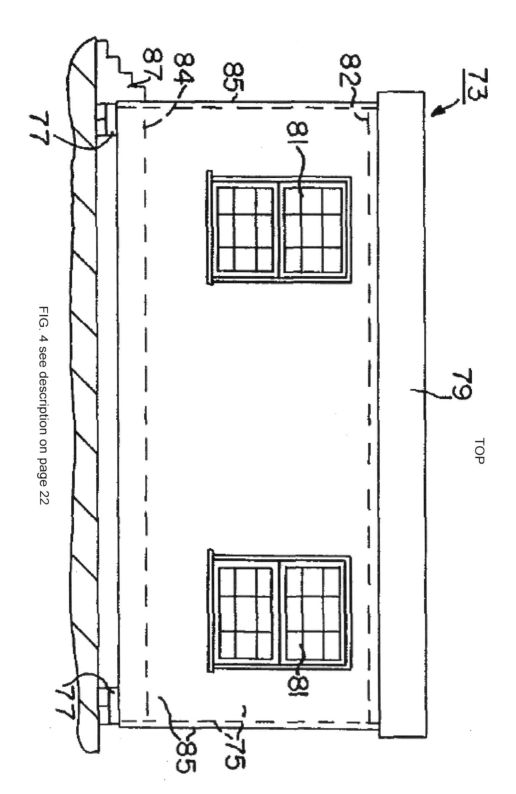

FIG. 4 see description on page 22

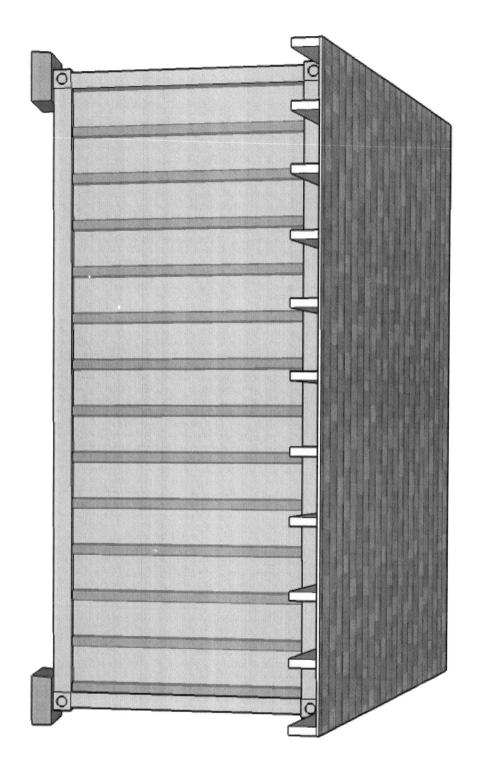

FIG. 5 is a front elevational view of a third embodiment of a novel building prepared by the novel method with two steel containers in spaced, side-by-side relationship.

26

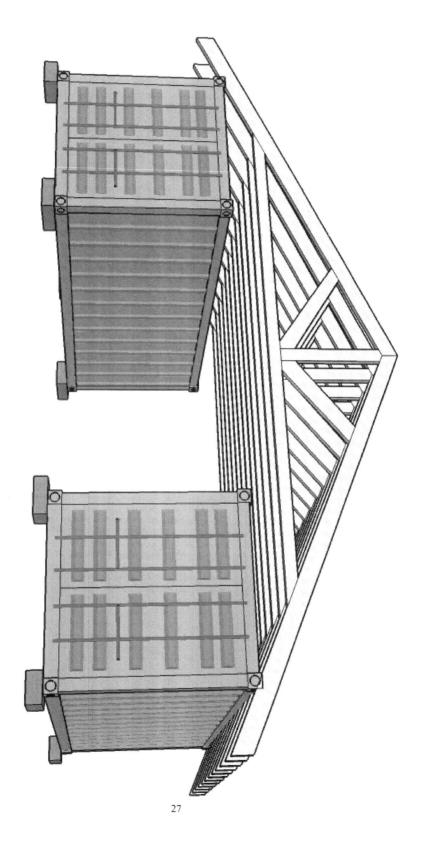

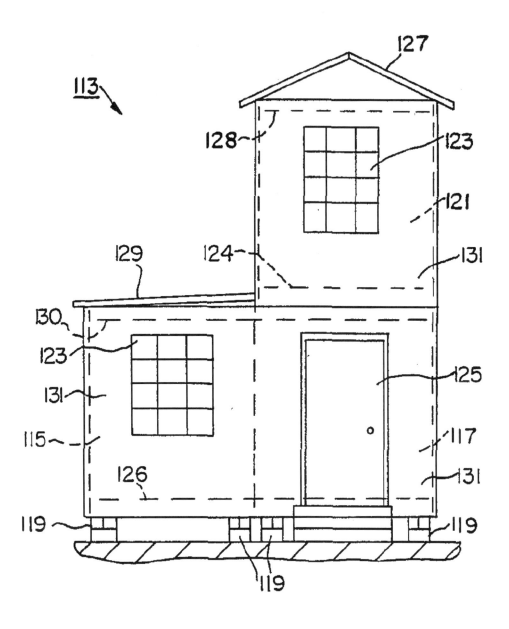

FIG. 6 is a front elevational view of a fourth embodiment of a novel building prepared by the novel method with one steel container mounted on top of one of two other steel container which are in abutting, side-by-side relationship.

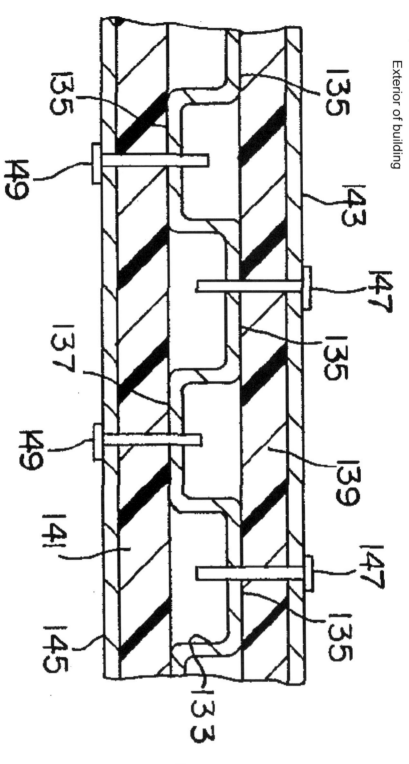

Exterior of building

135

143

147

135

137

149

139

141

145

147

135

133

149

135

FIG. 7 is a sectional view through a fragment of a sidewall of a novel building showing one form of construction employing thermal insulation, a decorative inner layer and a weather-resistant outer layer.

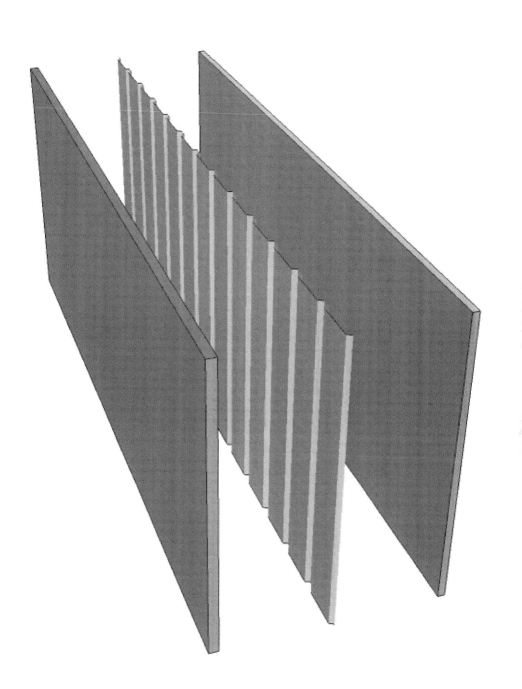

3 Detailed Description

Detailed Description of the Invention Including the Preferred Embodiments

The following description of some of the preferred embodiments of the concepts of this invention is made in reference to the accompanying figures. Where an individual structural element is depicted in more than one figure, it is assigned a common reference numeral for simplification of identification and understanding.

The novel method employs one or more standard steel shipping containers as a starting point for producing a structurally strong shell for a building. As pointed out above, such containers which have been taken out of service are used in the novel method, although new, unused containers can also be used.

Steel shipping containers are available in standard sizes, all of which are about eight (8) feet wide, eight and one half (81/2) feet high and different unit lengths including twenty (20) foot lengths and forty (40) foot lengths. They are of a welded steel construction for strength and to prevent pilferage. The containers are "standard" because they conform in size and construction to ISO or similar standards. Containers of any standard size may be used in the novel method and, for any particular building, the containers may all be the same size or may be different sizes.

Referring to FIG. 1, each container (21) and (23) includes a steel frame comprising a plurality of steel beams (27) welded together to form a rectangular parallelapiped. Each corner of the container has a metal fitting (29) with three connected holes in their outer faces, which fitting is adapted for stringing cables or ropes therethrough. These fittings may be used for anchoring the containers to one another and/or to the foundation. Where each container is mounted, it is mounted on its corner fittings so that the weight of the container and its contents is distributed in its steel frame.

Each container (21) and (23) includes (i) two opposed sidewalls (31) of corrugated steel sheet that is welded along its edges to the frame; (ii) a top wall (33) of light steel sheet welded around its edges to the frame; (iii) a bottom wall (35) of steel channel cross members with wood planks wedged therebetween and (iv) two opposed end walls, one endwall (37) being of corrugated steel welded along its edges to the frame and the other endwall comprising a double steel door (39) hinged at its edges to the frame.

FIG.I

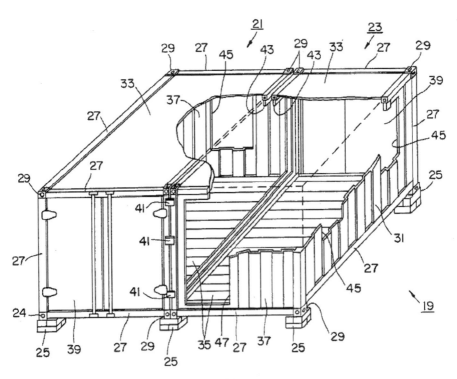

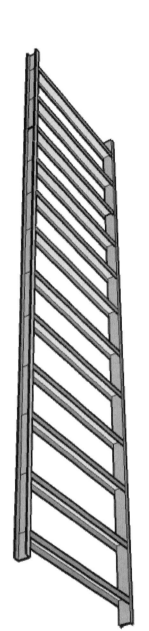

TOP

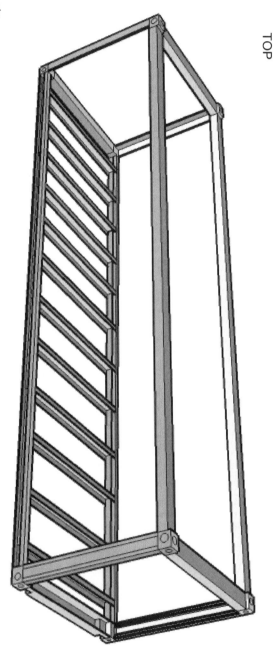

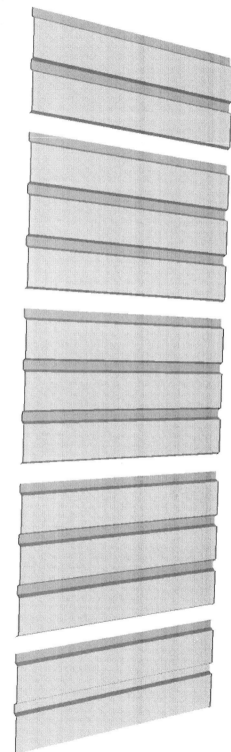

2.0 mm Panel
Thickness

1.6 mm Panel
Thickness

1.6 mm Panel
Thickness

1.6 mm Panel
Thickness

2.0 mm Panel
Thickness

Side Wall Components

Side walls are made from a series of smaller seamlessly welded corrugated panels (per side). The two outer panels (per side) are of a thicker steel (as shown) creating additional strength and rigidity.

Example 1

FIG. 1 illustrates the shell (19) for a building comprising two modified steel containers mounted on weight-bearing foundations in adjacent, abutting side-by-side relationship.

To prepare this shell, two standard steel twenty (20) foot containers (21) and (23) are first mounted on concrete-block footers (25) at the corners thereof in an adjacent, abutting side-by-side relationship. After the containers (21) and (23) have been mounted on the footers (25), they are welded together at their end walls with steel straps (41). Instead of welding, the two containers (21) and (23) may be joined together with bolts through their adjacent inner sidewalls. Substantially all of the adjacent inner sidewalls (31) are removed by cutting, as with an acetylene torch, except for narrow flanges (43) about four (4) to eight (8) inches long extending inwardly from the edges of the sidewalls and frame. It is advisable to retain these flanges (43) in order to retain an optimum amount of strength in the central frame members (27) of the building.

Window openings (45) and a door opening (47) are cut in the corrugated steel sheet of the endwalls (37) and the sidewalls (31). As described above, at least a narrow flange about four (4) to eight (8) inches long if left below the door opening (47) and above the door and window openings (45). The container doors in the endwalls (39) are closed and clamped, bolted or welded shut.

FIG. 1 shows the novel building at the point in construction where the containers (21) and (23) have been positioned on weight-bearing foundations and modified to form the shell of the building, but nothing has been added to the shell.

FIG.I

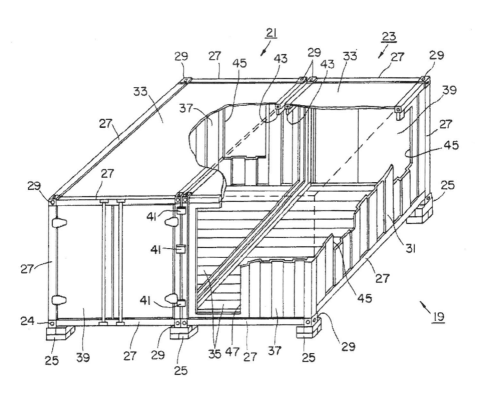

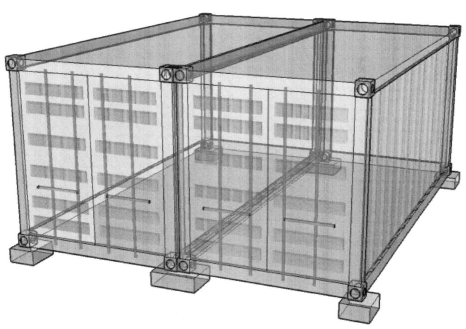

39

As shown in FIG. 2, various materials are added to the shell to complete the building (49). These additions adapt the building for its intended purpose and make the building more habitable. Generally, the installations of the various materials follow the usual practices in the construction of frame houses and of commercial buildings. However, some new methods may take advantage of or adapt to the character of the shell.

Roof trusses (51) are attached to the frame over the top walls (33) and a roof (53) of sheet plywood, asphalt-impregnated paper, and roofing shingles are installed thereon. Of course, other roof designs maybe used. After the roof is (53) installed, electrical service, plumbing, and other services are installed. Because of the corrugated character of the sidewalls (31) and endwalls (37), the pipes, wires and fixtures of the various services may be installed in the corrugations of these walls.

Windows and window frames (55) are installed in the window openings (45) shown in FIG. 1. A door and a door frame (not shown) is installed in the door opening (47) shown in FIG. 1. A raised floor (57) is installed over the bottom walls (35) using wood spacers (59) in such manner as to enclose the flanges (43) extending inwardly from the bottom wall (35). A dropped ceiling (61) is installed under the top walls (33) using spacers (63) in such manner as to enclose the flanges (43) which extend inwardly from the top wall (33). Steps or a ramp (not shown) installed outside the building from ground level to each outside door.

Optionally, stud walls (not shown) may be installed within the building (49) to divide the floor space therein into two or more rooms. Interior finished walls (65) are constructed on the sidewalls (31) and end walls (37) and (39) using spacers (67), and also on interior stud walls if present. Where the flanges (43) protrude, they may be enclosed with a box (69) carrying the interior finish. A baseboard (71) may also be installed. The outer surfaces of the building are covered with a layer of foam insulation and a layer of weather-resistant material (70) as described below with respect to FIG. 7.

Various appliances, such as a water-heater, a space heater, an airconditioner, a range, an over, a dish washer, a clothes washer, a clothes dryer, etc. maybe installed in the same way as they are commonly installed in other buildings. In fact, an advantage of the novel building is that it can be completed using methods that are compatible with or identical with current building practice. Yet the shell can be produced on-site by the novel modification of two or more out-of-service standard steel shipping containers.

FIG.1

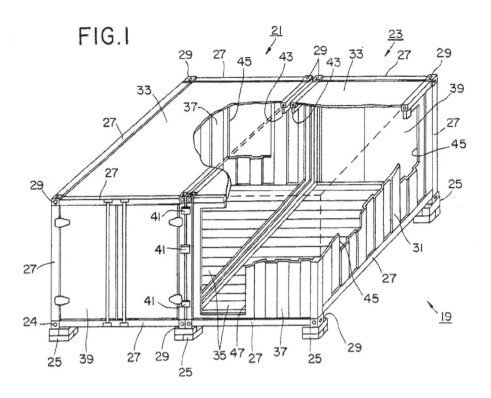

FIG.2

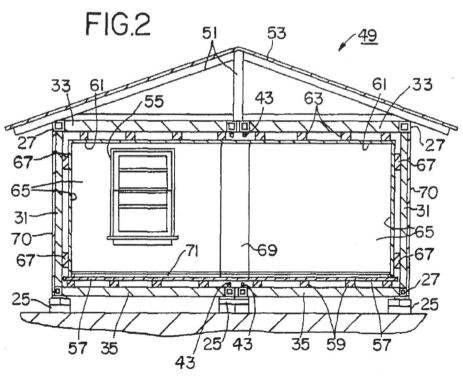

Example 2

The novel method may be used to prepare a novel habitable building (73) from only one steel shipping container (75) as exemplified by the second embodiment shown in FIGS. 3 and 4.

Fabrication of the novel building (73) follows the procedure described in Example 1, except that only one container is used and, therefore, the steps of joining two containers together and removing facing portions of adjacent inner sidewalls is unnecessary.

The single container (75) is mounted at the ends thereof on concrete block footers (77) or other weight-bearing foundation. A roof (79) is installed over the topwall of the container (75). Window openings and a door opening are cut out of the steel sidewalls and endwalls of the container (75). Then, windows (81) and a door (83) are installed in these openings. A dropped ceiling (82) and a raised floor (84) are installed inside the container as described in Example 1.

A layer of outside thermal insulation is installed adjacent the outside surfaces of the container (75), and then a weather-resistant layer (85) is installed on the outside insulation layer as shown in FIG. 7. A layer of inside thermal insulation (not shown) is installed adjacent the inside surfaces of the sidewalls and endwalls of the container (75) and then a decorative layer is installed on the inside insulation layer, as shown in FIG. 7.

Outside steps (87) leading up to the door (83) are also provided. As in Example 1, inside partitions, doors, closets and various services and appliances are installed inside the shell as desired.

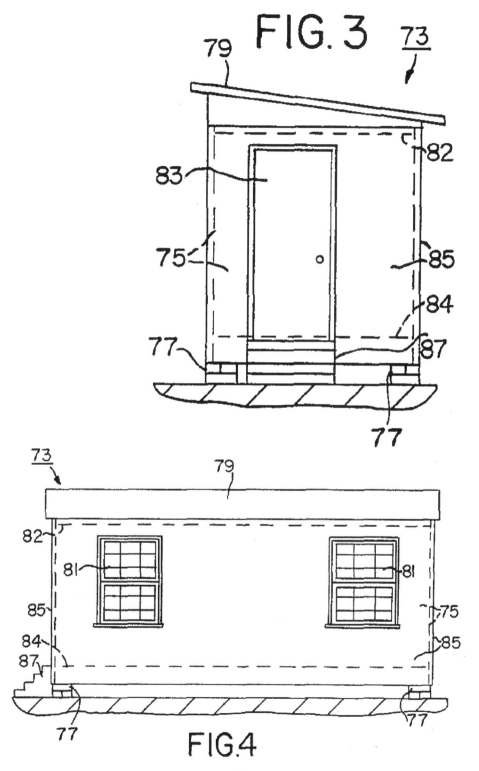

FIG. 3

FIG.4

Example 3

The novel method may be used to prepare a novel habitable building (89) from two steel shipping containers (91A) and (91B) that are mounted in spaced-apart side-by-side relationship, as exemplified by the third embodiment shown in FIG. 5.

Fabrication of the novel building (89) follows the procedure described in Example 1, except that the containers (91) are spaced apart, the space therebetween is enclosed, and access means are provided between the enclosed space and each of the containers. The steps of joining the two containers and removing facing portions of adjacent inner sidewalls described in Example 1 is unnecessary.

In the third embodiment shown in FIG. 5, each container (91A) and (91B) is mounted at the ends thereof on concrete-block footers (93) or other weight-bearing foundations. The distance between the containers (91A) and (91B) can be any desired amount. In this example, the containers are spaced apart about ten (10) feet.

A subframe (95) comprising metal or wood headers and joists are assembled on top of the footers (93) that are under the inside sidewalls (96A) and (96B) of the containers (91A) and (91B). Spacer beams (97) are attached at the upper edges of the inside sidewalls (96A) and (96B) bridging the space therebetween to complete the frame of the shell and to maintain the containers in proper relationship to one another.

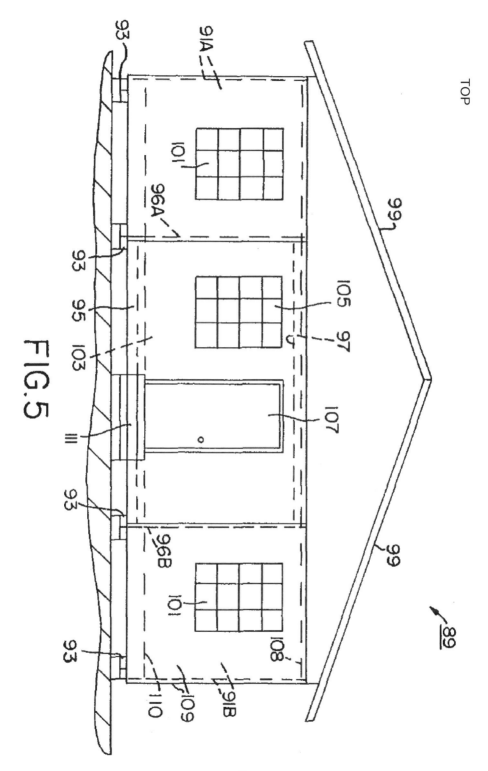

TOP

FIG.5

89

A common roof (99) including roof trusses (not shown) is installed over the topwalls of the containers (91A) and (91B) and the space therebetween.

Window openings and a door opening may be cut out of the steel sidewalls and endwalls of the containers (91A) and (91B). Then windows (101) and a door (not shown) may be installed in these openings.

A stud wall (103) is constructed at each end of the space between the containers (91A) and (91B) to complete the closure of said space. The stud walls (103) may include windows (105) and a door (107). The space defined by the subframe (95), the roof (99) and the stud walls (103) becomes living space which, because of its construction, increases living space without adding to the number of steel containers that are required.

Access openings (not shown) are cut out of the inside sidewalls (96A) and (96B) to provide access between the enclosed space and each of the containers.

As in Example 1, a dropped ceiling (108) and a raised floor (110) are installed inside the containers (91A) and (91B) and in the space therebetween. A layer of outside thermal insulation is installed against the outside surfaces of the shell, and then a weather-resistant layer (109) is installed thereon (see FIG. 7.). A layer of inside thermal insulation is installed against the inside surfaces of the shell, and then a decorative layer (see FIG. 7) is installed thereon.

Outside steps (111) leading up to the door (107) are also provided. As in Example 1, inside partitions, doors, closets and various services and appliances are installed inside the shell as desired.

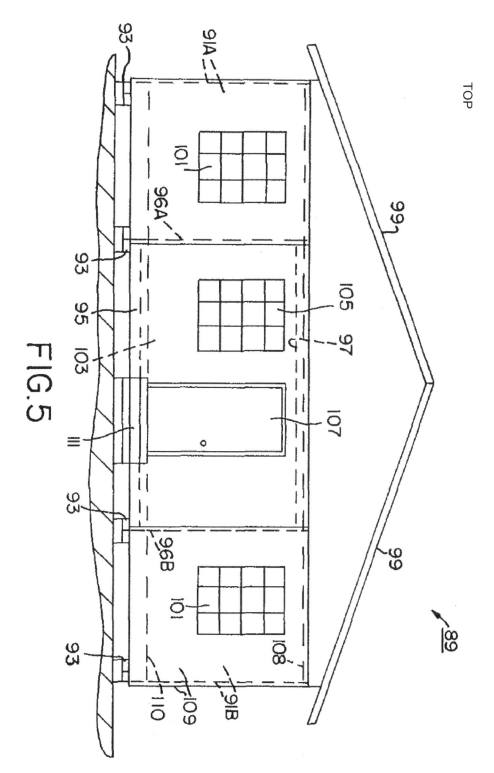

FIG.5

TOP

89

Example 4

The novel method may be used to prepare a novel habitable building (113) by placing one or more shipping containers on top of one or more containers at ground level.

In the fourth embodiment shown in FIG. 6, two steel shipping containers (115) and (117) are mounted in concrete-block foundations (119) in abutting, side-by-side relationship, similar to the arrangements shown in FIG. 1. Then, a third steel shipping container (121) is mounted on top of and in alignment with one of the steel shipping containers (117), with the corner blocks of the upper container (121) on the corner blocks of the lower container (117).

The containers (115), (117) and (121) are then connected together as by welding, strapping or bolting or any other method which will retain the physical relationship among them. Portions of the sidewalls and endwalls of the three containers are removed to provide access between the lower containers (115) and (117), and to provide window and door openings in all three containers. In addition, a portion of the top wall of the one lower container (117) and also the opposite portion of the bottom wall of the upper container (121) is removed to provide an opening for a stair (not shown).

As in the foregoing examples, windows (123) and doors (125) are installed in the window and door openings and a stair (not shown) is installed in the stair opening between the raised floor (124) of the upper container (121) and the raised floor (126) of the one lower container (117).

A roof (127) is installed over the upper container (121). A deck (129) (or another roof in the alternative) is installed over the other lower container (115). Dropped ceilings (128) and (130), and raised floors (124) and (126), are installed in lower and upper containers. Inside and outside insulation layers are installed on inside and outside surfaces of the containers as described below with respect to FIG. 7. A weather-resistant layer (131) is installed on the outside insulation layer and a decorative layer is installed on the inside insulation layer (see FIG. 7).

As in Example 1, inside partitions, doors, closets and various services and appliances are installed as desired.

FIG.6

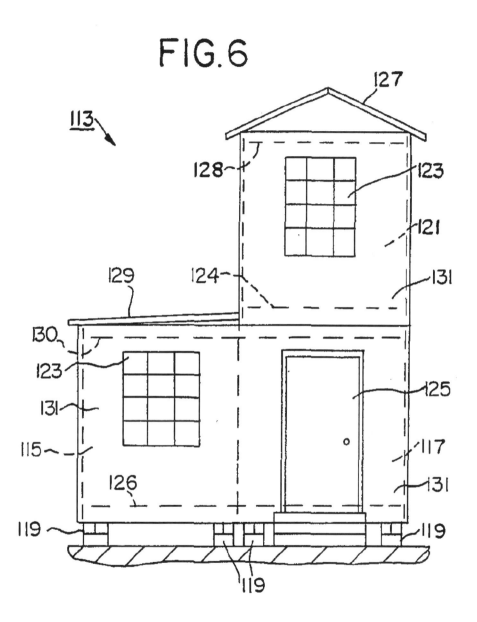

FIG. 7 shows one construction of an outside wall for any of the foregoing embodiments, which construction is simple, is effective for making the building habitable, and can be assembled with low labor cost.

The corrugated steel wall (133) is cleaned and a temporary adhesive is applied to the outside and inside raised surfaces (135) and (137).

Then, outside and inside plastic foam sheets (139) and (141) respectively of thermal insulation are pressed against and adhered to the raised surfaces (135) and (137) respectively.

Sheets of weather-resistant material (143) are held against the outside insulation layer (139) while holes are drilled through the outside layers (143) and, (139) and the outside raised portions (135); and connectors (147) are attached to the outside raised portion (135).

Similarly, sheets of decorative inside material (145) are held against the inside insulation layer (141) while holes are drilled through the inside layers (145) and, (141) and the inside raised portions (137); and connectors (149) are attached to the inside raised portions (137). The decorative layer is preferably wood panels or sheet-rock panels.

This construction reduces heat transfer through the walls to improve habitability in both hot and cold environments. In some constructions, it may be desirable to include a vapor barrier adjacent the outer insulation layer.

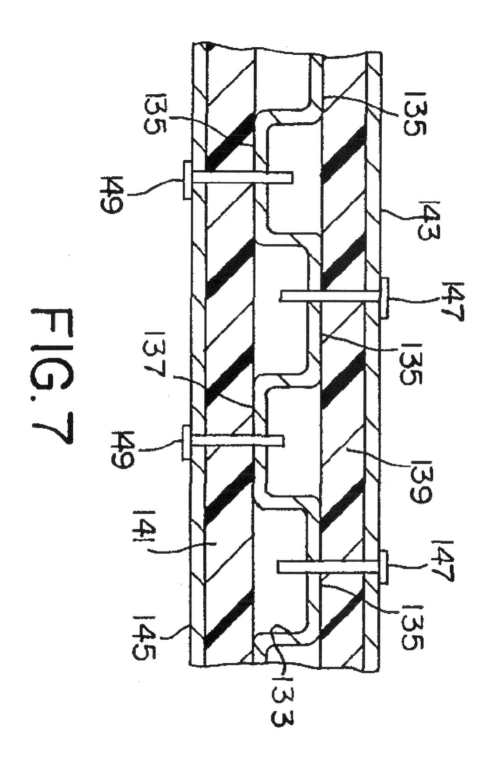

FIG.7

In addition to mounting steel containers as described in the examples, one or more containers may be mounted with one end partially in the ground. For instance, FIG. 6 may be modified so that one ends of the lower containers (115) and (117) are mounted as shown and the other far end of the lower containers are mounted in the ground so that the far end (not shown) of the upper container (121) has direct access to ground level by way of another short set of steps.

In still other arrangements; one or more steel containers may be mounted in the ground under and in alignment with the ground level steel containers to thereby provide a cellar for the building. This arrangement is particularly practical in dry climates with well drained soil.

It is noteworthy that the novel building is expandable. For instance, another steel container can be added to an existing novel building in abutting or in spaced, side-by-side relationship in the manner described above. In another instance, another steel container may be added on top of the container of an existing building provided the foundation is strong enough.

As pointed out above, the containers can be used to ship to the building site the additional parts for upgrading the building. Additional space in the container can be used to ship other, unrelated goods, thereby reducing the cost of the container to the builder.

Also, where several novel buildings are to be built at the same location, one or more containers can be used temporarily as the builders office and/or warehouse for parts while the novel buildings are being built.

FIG.6

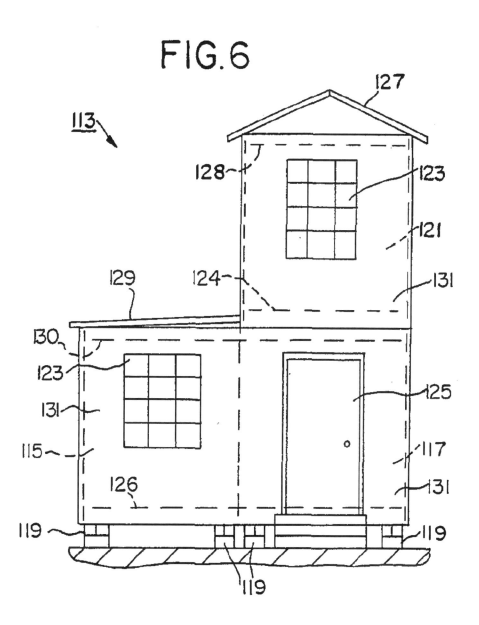

Download 3D models of original diagrams at www.paulsawyers.com

4 Expanded Discussion

Expanding on the Clark patent description could take one in a number of different directions ranging from minor to large scale modifications or additions to the structures originally shown. For example, in regards to Figure 6 the three-container building, a fourth container could be added at ground level along with a steeply pitched roof to create a pyramid or A-frame shaped structure. The stackable nature of shipping containers combined with traditional roof building techniques, and methods derived from the Clark invention, can produce a surprising number of building variations.

The Clark patent describes an effective and repeatable method of creating shipping container buildings, of which the following pages expand on with several basic building techniques that can serve to complement the inventions main summary description which states (that the method comprises):

The mounting of at least one standard steel shipping container on a weight-bearing foundation.

Two or more containers can also be used, with the containers placed in an abutting or spaced side-by-side relationship.

All, or portions of the inner sidewalls can be removed when containers are mounted side-by-side creating passageways or a larger open interior space.

Truss or rafter built gable style roofing can be installed mounted on the top side rails of the containers to protect the structure from weather.

Floor joists and decking can be installed over the existing plywood floor of the container enclosing flanges and creating a space where foam board insulation can be installed.

Small hooks can be tack-welded to the underside of container roof panels and a grid style fiber panel dropped ceiling installed (suspended by wires) enclosing flanges that extend inwardly from the top walls and creating a space for foam board or roll fiberglass insulation.

At least one opening (for a door) can be cut into the side or end wall, and a door installed by use of welded-on angle iron, a 2x4 frame, shims and screws. Glass sliding doors, roll-up doors, and additional windows can also be installed.

Concrete Footings and Piers

Setting up a shipping container building begins with site preparation (grading, drainage, etc if required), followed by the installation of any permanent concrete footings that may be employed. The Clark patent description mentions "concrete block footers" as the type of footings called for, so poured footings are not necessarily a requirement, but buildings located in cold climates would certainly benefit from a footing that extends below the frost line.

Pre-made concrete piers and adjustable concrete piers would also be effective if placed in a larger quantity under the lower side rails, cross members, and corner fittings (say perhaps every four feet). Additionally, when a building will have large portions of side wall material removed, as pointed out, a loss of rigidity will always occur along the floor of abutting containers. This situation will almost certainly dictate the use of adjustable concrete piers placed strategically throughout the under side of the joined container sections to reinstate any lost firmness.

Less advanced container buildings that are to receive no removal of side wall material (save for perhaps a standard size door and window) can be adequately supported on a foundation of four custom poured footings, one under each steel corner fitting. The dimension of each of these footings should be somewhat oversized to support the concentration of weight (16-24 inches square and to the depth required for frost line - or 16"x48" concrete form tubes for round footings).

Also, an optional custom made steel anchor plate assembly can be embedded into wet concrete footings allowing you to weld-down the corner fittings after placement.

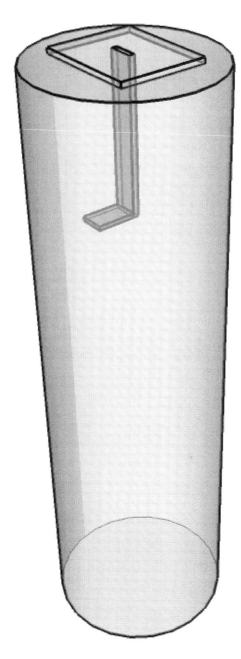

Concrete form tube 16 inch diameter x 4 feet long. This standard length tube can be cut down to pour a shorter footing for warmer climates. Frost depth normally dictates footing depth requirements. 8 inch x 8 inch square 1/4 inch steel plate with welded-on j-hook is submerged in concrete creating a strong anchoring platform that the bottom corner fittings can be joined to via welds.

Welding and Bolting Containers Together

Once paired containers are placed in a permanent position, fine adjustments to level are made on footings using steel plate shims and containers are welded together using 1/4 inch or thicker steel plate straps. The Clark patent specifies positioning straps over the end walls... a more detailed specification would be "over the abutted (113 x 40 x 12 mm) corner posts". Welding anchor plates over the corner fittings is also an option, but many builders prefer to retain the industrial shipping container aesthetics by leaving the corner fittings exposed.

If a multi-container building is planned in a side-by-side layout without the addition of a lumber built roof, welding a continual strap of thinner 1/8 inch plate steel across the abutting top side rails (that can later be coated with an asphalt based roofing cement) will keep water from draining into the structure. If a lumber built roof is planned, the gaps between top side rails and corner posts can be filled with expanding foam, or a sheathing material, but a continual panel of various gauge plate steel remains the most preferable method.

The Clark method describes an alternative method of bolting containers together through the perimeter of side walls prior to the central section (of side walls) being trimmed out and removed. This method requires builders to keep a 4-8 inch border of side wall material that is anchored together using common hardware store bolts nuts and washers (3/8-1/2 inch bolts installed in holes drilled every 16-24 inches through both abutting side walls). As mentioned, the remaining flanges will extend 4-8 inches into the usable space of the building interior. Welding containers remains the superior method as side wall material can be trimmed out completely creating a floor, ceiling, and end walls with a nearly flush profile (although a small flange created by the exposed frame rails and posts will remain).

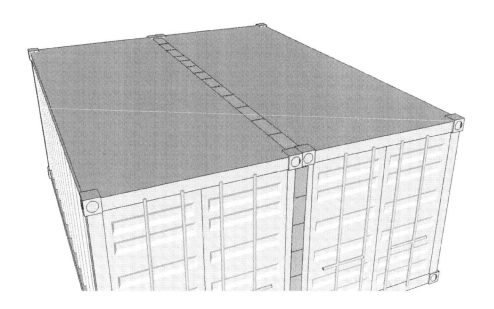

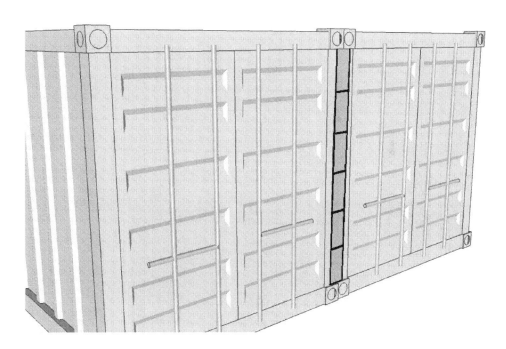

Plate steel welded over the gaps is a common method of joining steel shipping containers into one large box-like structure. Both end and top-side joined seams are covered in the above illustrations.

Cutting Steel Shipping Containers

Cutting the steel wall material of shipping containers in regard to the Clark Patent involves two procedures: 1) side wall removal from inside, 2) cutting door and window openings.

Steel shipping containers have 1.6mm - 2.0mm thick side walls. This variation of thickness is further described on page 37.

The 1.6mm thick front end wall can also be cut-out for door installations as seen in the photo on page 15.

<u>Effective Cutting Tools</u>
- Plasma cutter
- Metal cutting circular saw
- Reciprocating saw with 24 TPI metal cutting blade
- Angle grinder (abrasive cutter with ultra thin discs)
- Acetylene torch

The Clark Patent instructions describe connecting containers together first before removing side wall material from the interior. Large segments of side wall steel are heavy and difficult to handle. Taking this into account, it's easier to cut side wall material in smaller 2-4 foot wide segments then remove these pieces via the cargo doors.

It's best to finish raw cut door and window openings with welded-on angle iron to create a flush surface. This allows for easy mounting of a 2x4 frame. Once a 2x4 frame is in place you can install doors and windows in the traditional manner using shims and screws. Cut openings large enough to accommodate a) welded-on angle iron, b) 2x4 frame that bolts to angle iron, c) shims, and d) pre-hung door or window. Make certain you have guaranteed your dimensions are properly figured prior to making any cuts as you will not be able to easily repair incorrect cut-outs.

Side Wall and Related Component Specifications

Typical Steel Dry Cargo Shipping Container

40 Foot Model

Top Side Rails
Each top side rail is a 60 x 60 x 3.0 mm square steel pipe.

Bottom Side Rails
Qty : 2
Shape : Channel Section
Dimension : 162 x 48 x 30 x 4.5 mm

Side Walls
a) Inner panel : 1.6 mm thick (9 panels each side)
b) Outer panel : 2.0 mm thick (2 panels each side)
c) Corrugation shape:
Outer face : 72 mm , Slope : 68 mm
Inner face : 70 mm , Depth : 36 mm

Front End Wall
Thickness: 1.6 mm
Corrugation dimension- Outer face : 110 mm , Depth : 45.6 mm
Inner face : 104 mm , Slope : 18 mm

20 Foot Model

Top Side Rails
Each top side rail is a 60 x 60 x 3.0 mm square steel pipe.

Bottom Side Rails
Qty : 2
Shape : Channel Section
Dimension : 158 x 48 x 30 x 4.5mm

Side Walls
a) Inner panels : 1.6 mm thick
b) Outer panels : 2.0 mm thick

Front End Wall
Thickness: 1.6 mm
Corrugation dimension- Outer face : 110 mm , Depth : 45.6 mm
Inner face : 104 mm , Slope : 18 mm

Roofing Details

Successful (supplementary) shipping container roofs built using tradition truss or rafter methods require a strong anchor point that must first be created along the shipping container top rails and/or upper portions of the side wall. Truss and rafter anchoring methods can vary greatly in design. The two methods described in this publication utilize simple commonly available dimensional lumber and standard hardware store fasteners.

Anchoring 2x4 Truss Mounting Platform Using Welded-on Steel Brackets

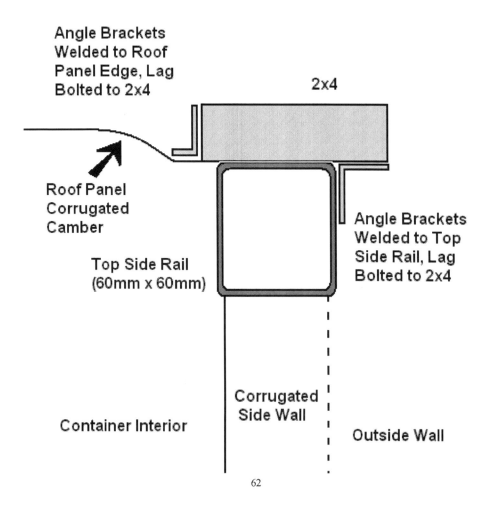

Angle Brackets Welded to Roof Panel Edge, Lag Bolted to 2x4

2x4

Roof Panel Corrugated Camber

Angle Brackets Welded to Top Side Rail, Lag Bolted to 2x4

Top Side Rail (60mm x 60mm)

Corrugated Side Wall

Container Interior

Outside Wall

No-Weld Truss Mounting Platform

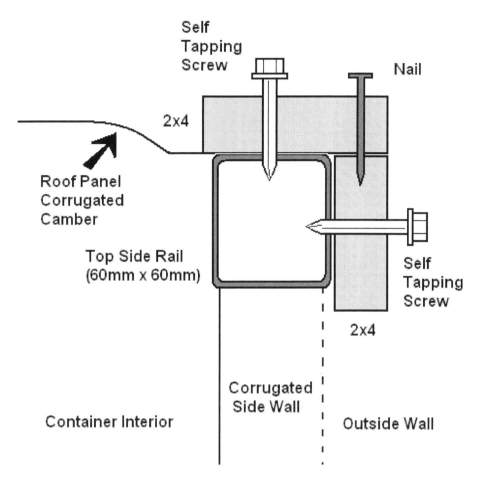

The top side rail contains a weld bead where the roof panels connect that may prevent a perfectly flush seating of lumber. You can install shims every 16 inches in any gaps to create a level surface if needed.

Small portions of truss mounting lumber may require removal using a wood chisel and hammer to clear corner fittings and so forth.

Three container building note: on lower roof, rafters can be anchored easily to the second story containers side-wall by way of a simple through-bolted ledger (bolted to the side-wall of upper-level container using 3/8 (minimum) galvanized bolts, washers, and lock washers, every 24 inches)

Raised Floor and Dropped Ceiling

The Clark patent describes the installation of a raised floor and a dropped ceiling primarily for the purpose of concealing the flange that remains after removing side-wall material. This flange must be kept longer if bolting containers together to provide an adequate bolting area (a 4-8 inch border of side wall material is retained for this purpose), while containers that are joined via welds will have a much smaller flange consisting of the remaining exposed framework components as sidewall material is trimmed-out flush to the frame.

Besides this main purpose of covering a flange, the raised floor and dropped ceiling can also serve to: a) cover an existing shipping container plywood floor that is dirty, impregnated with pesticide, or in otherwise rough condition. b) create a small pocket of space between the existing floor and ceiling, and the new floor and ceiling for foam board insulation placement.

The raised floor should be built with 2x2, 2x4, 2x6, or 2x8 floor joists (depending on the height of the flange to be covered). Space floor joists 16" oc, drill and countersink for screws if using 2x2's (use brackets for larger dimensions lumber), and screw joists directly to the containers existing 28mm thick plywood. Install foam board insulation between joists, followed by 3/4" plywood sheets as the new flooring over joists.

The Clark patent describes installation of a drop ceiling that utilizes spacers, and perhaps drywall, although this is not specified. While a wood framework of studs for mounting drywall on the ceiling could certainly be constructed, a faster method would be to install a common fiber panel drop ceiling. These are quick and inexpensive to install, and offer a nice finished look, consisting of metal grid-work suspended on wires from small hooks tack-welded to the containers roof panels.

Drop ceiling fiber panels (available in 2×2 or 2×4 foot sizes and a variety of colors and textures) are then installed within the grid. The fiber panels alone will provide a certain amount of insulation, but additional foam board panels or fiberglass roll insulation should be placed above the drop ceiling to maximize interior comfort. Lighting fixtures that mount directly into the ceiling grid are also readily available.

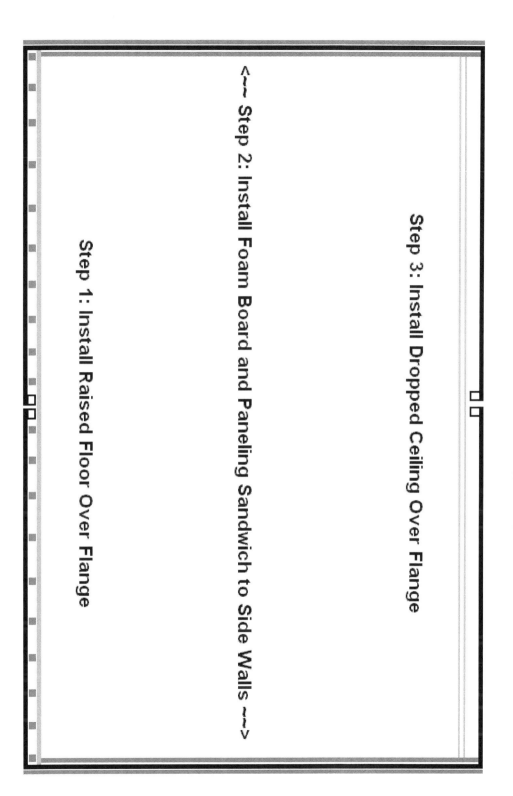

Step 3: Install Dropped Ceiling Over Flange

<~~ Step 2: Install Foam Board and Paneling Sandwich to Side Walls ~~>

Step 1: Install Raised Floor Over Flange

MCKU 2014850

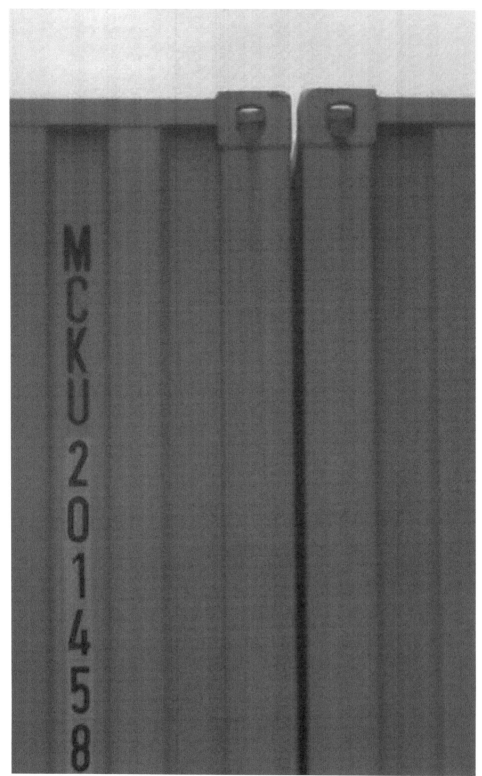

5 Shipping Container Specifications

Typical 40 ft Steel Dry Cargo Shipping Container

40 ft Long x 8 ft Wide x 8.5 ft High

External Dimensions
Length 40' (12,192 mm)
Width 8' (2,438 mm)
Height 8'6" (2,591 mm)

Internal Dimensions
Length 39' 4 13/64" (12,032 mm)
Width 7' 8 33/64" (2,350 mm)
Height 7'10 3/32" (2,390 mm)

Door Opening Dimension
Width 7' 8 3/64" (2,338 mm)
Height 7' 5 49/64" (2,280 mm)

Internal Cubic Capacity
2390 cu. ft (67.7 cu. m)

Empty Weight
8,070 lbs (3,660 kg)

Maximum Payload
59,130 lbs (26,820 kg)

Gooseneck Tunnel Dimensions
Length 3,315 mm
Width 1,029 mm
Height/depth 120 mm

Typical 40 ft Steel Dry Cargo Shipping Container

Component Dimensions

Bottom Side Rails
Qty : 2
Shape : Channel Section
Dimension : 162 x 48 x 30 x 4.5 mm

Crossmembers
Shape : " C " section
Small one : 122 x 45 x 40 x 4.0 mm , Qty : 25
Large one : 122 x 75 x 40 x 4.0 mm , Qty : 3

Gooseneck Tunnel Parts (40ft only)
a) Tunnel plate thickness : 4.0 mm Qty : 1
b) Tunnel bow thickness : 4.0 mm Qty : 12
c) Bolster thickness: 150 x 100 x 4.0 mm, Qty : 1
d) Outriggers - "C" section: 118 x 75 x 40 x 4.0 mm, Qty : 1/each,
Side 118 x 45 x 40 x 4.0 mm, Qty : 7/each side

Front End Wall
Thickness: 1.6 mm
Corrugation dimension- Outer face : 110 mm , Depth : 45.6 mm
Inner face : 104 mm , Slope : 18 mm

Front End Frame
Consists of one front sill, two corner posts, one front header and
four corner castings.

Front Sill
Consists of "L" section steel and a square tube front rail on top.
"L" section plate : 4.0 mm thick.
Front rail : 60 x 60 x 3.0 mm

Corner Post
 Corner posts are made using 6.0 mm thick section steel.

Front Header
Lower rail : 60 x 60 x 3.0 mm
Upper part : 3.0 mm thick

Typical 40 ft Steel Dry Cargo Shipping Container

Component Dimensions

Rear End
Consists of one door sill, two corner posts, one rear header with header plate and four corner fittings, and the doors.

Door Sill
a) Door sill : 4.5 mm thick Slope : 1:10 approx.
b) Stiffener ribs : 4.5 mm thick Qty : 4 Pcs.

Corner Post
Inner part : 113 x 40 x 12 mm
Outer part : 6.0 mm thick

Door Header
Rear header : 4.0 mm thick
Header plate : 3.0 mm thick
Rib : 4.0 mm thick , Qty : 4

Door Assembly
Two door leaves, two locking devices, four hinges and pins, seal gaskets and the door holders. The doors are capable of opening 270 degrees.

Door Leaves
1) Door panel :
Depth : 36 mm
Inner face : 72 mm
Slope : 68 mm
Panel thickness : 2.0 mm

2) Door frame :
a) Vertical door member: 100 x 50 x 3.2 mm
b) Horizontal door member: 150 x 50 x 3.0 mm

Typical 40 ft Steel Dry Cargo Shipping Container

Component Dimensions

Side Wall Components

Top Side Rails
Each top side rail is a 60 x 60 x 3.0 mm square steel pipe.

Side Walls
a) Inner panel : 1.6 mm thick (9 panels each side)
b) Outer panel : 2.0 mm thick (2 panels each side)
c) Corrugation shape:
Outer face : 72 mm , Slope : 68 mm
Inner face : 70 mm , Depth : 36 mm

Roof Panels
Corrugation Shape - Depth : 20 mm , Pitch : 209 mm
Inter face : 91 mm , Slope : 13.5 mm
Outer face : 91 mm
Camber upwards : 5 mm
Panel thickness : 2.0 mm
Sheet Qty : 11 Pcs

Roof Reinforcement Plates
Four 3.0 m thick reinforcement plates are be mounted around the four corner fittings.

Protrusions of Corner Fittings Beyond Container Body
Shipping containers are measured at the longest and widest points. These points are the corner fittings which extend slightly beyond the body of the container as follows.

a) The top of corner fittings protrude 6 mm above the highest point of the corrugated roof panel assembly.
b) The lower faces of the cross members are on a plane 17 mm above the lower faces of the bottom corner fittings.
c) The outside faces of corner fittings protrude from the outside faces of the corner post by 3 mm. The outside faces of the corner fittings protrude from the outside faces of the side walls by nominal 7 mm.

Typical 40 ft Steel Dry Cargo Shipping Container

Component Dimensions

Floor

The Floor Boards
Plywood treated with preservative (required by the Common-wealth Department of Health, Australia).
Plywood thickness : 28 mm
Plywood ply number : 19
Plywood material : Apitong, Keruing, (or other Asian hardwood)
Glue : Phenol-formaldehyde resin
Preservative: BASILEUM SI-84 or others

The plywood boards are secured to each crossmember with self-tapping zinc plated steel screws. The screws are countersunk 2 mm deep.
Screws : 8 mm diameter shank x 16 mm diameter head x 45 mm length

Typical 20 ft Steel Dry Cargo Shipping Container

20 ft Long x 8 ft Wide x 8.5 ft High

External Dimensions
Length 19'10 1/2" (6,058 mm)
Width 8' (2,438 mm)
Height 8'6" (2,591 mm)

Internal Dimensions
Length 19'4 13/64" (5,898 mm)
Width 7' 8 33/64" (2,350 mm)
Height 7'10 3/32" (2,390 mm)

Door Opening Dimension
Width 7' 8 3/64" (2,338 mm)
Height 7' 5 49/64" (2,280 mm)

Internal Cubic Capacity
1,170 cu. ft (33.1 cu. m)

Empty Weight
4,755 lbs (2,155 kg)

Maximum Payload
62,445 lbs (28,325 kg)

Typical 20 ft Steel Dry Cargo Shipping Container

Component Dimensions

Bottom Side Rails
Qty : 2
Shape : Channel Section
Dimension : 158 x 48 x 30 x 4.5 mm

Forklift Pockets
Most 20 ft containers have forklift pockets made from 3 mm and 6 mm thick steel. These pockets are built into the lower cross member assembly.

Crossmembers
Shape : " C " section
Small one : 122 x 40 x 40 x 4.0 mm , Qty : 16
Large one : 122 x 75 x 45 x 4.5 mm , Qty : 2

Front End Wall
Thickness: 1.6 mm
Corrugation dimension- Outer face : 110 mm , Depth : 45.6 mm
Inner face : 104 mm , Slope : 18 mm

Front End Frame
Consists of one front sill, two corner posts, one front header and four corner castings.

Front Sill
Consists of "L" section steel and a square tube front rail on top.
"L" section plate : 4.0 mm thick.
Front rail : 60 x 60 x 3.0 mm

Corner Post
Corner posts are made using 6.0 mm thick section steel.

Front Header
Lower rail : 60 x 60 x 3.0 mm
Upper part : 3.0 mm thick

Typical 20 ft Steel Dry Cargo Shipping Container

Component Dimensions

Rear End
Consists of one door sill, two corner posts, one rear header with header plate and four corner fittings, and the doors.

Corner Post
Inner part : 113 x 40 x 10 mm
Outer part : 6.0 mm thick

Door Header
Rear header : 4.0 mm thick
Header plate : 3.0 mm thick

Door Assembly
Two door leaves, two locking devices, four hinges and pins, seal gaskets and the door holders. The doors are capable of opening 270 degrees.

Door Leaves
1) Door panel :
thickness : 1.6 mm
2) Door frame :
a) Vertical door member: 100 x 50 x 3.2 mm
b) Horizontal door member: 150 x 50 x 3.0 mm

Side Wall Components

Top Side Rails
Each top side rail is a 60 x 60 x 3.0 mm square steel pipe.

Side Walls
a) Inner panels : 1.6 mm thick
b) Outer panels : 2.0 mm thick

Roof Panels
Camber upwards : 6 mm
Panel thickness : 1.6 mm
Sheet Qty : 5 Pcs

Typical 20 ft Steel Dry Cargo Shipping Container

Component Dimensions

Roof Reinforcement Plates
Four 3.0 m thick reinforcement plates are be mounted around the four corner fittings.

Protrusions of Corner Fittings Beyond Container Body
Shipping containers are measured at the longest and widest points. These points are the corner fittings which extend slightly beyond the body of the container as follows.

a) The top of corner fittings protrude 6 mm above the highest point of the corrugated roof panel assembly.
b) The lower faces of the cross members are on a plane 12.5 mm +5/-1.5 mm above the lower faces of the bottom corner fittings.
c) The outside faces of corner fittings protrude from the outside faces of the corner post by 4 mm. The outside faces of the corner fittings protrude from the outside faces of the side walls by nominal 8 mm.

Floor

The Floor Boards
Plywood treated with preservative (required by the Commonwealth Department of Health, Australia).
Plywood thickness : 28 mm
Plywood ply number : 19
Plywood material : Apitong, Keruing, (or other Asian hardwood)
Glue : Phenol-formaldehyde resin
Preservative: BASILEUM SI-84 or others

The plywood boards are secured to each crossmember with self-tapping zinc plated steel screws. The screws are countersunk 2 mm deep.
Screws : 8 mm diameter shank x 16 mm diameter head x 45 mm length

Made in the USA
Lexington, KY
26 January 2012